# DOGS SET V

# Bloodhounds

Julie Murray
ABDO Publishing Company

Published by ABDO Publishing Company, 4940 Viking Drive, Edina, Minnesota 55435.
Copyright © 2003 by Abdo Consulting Group, Inc. International copyrights reserved in
all countries. No part of this book may be reproduced in any form without written
permission from the publisher.

Printed in the United States.

Cover Photo: Ron Kimball
Interior Photos: Corbis pp. 5, 9; Ron Kimball pp. 7, 11, 13, 15, 17, 19, 21

Contributing Editors: Kate A. Conley, Kristin Van Cleaf, Kristianne E. Vieregger
Art Direction & Graphics: Neil Klinepier

### Library of Congress Cataloging-in-Publication Data

Murray, Julie, 1969-
    Bloodhounds / Julie Murray.
       p. cm. -- (Dogs. Set V)
    Summary: An introduction to the physical characteristics, behavior, and proper care
of Bloodhounds.
    Includes bibliographical references (p. ).
    ISBN 1-57765-920-1
    1. Bloodhound--Juvenile literature. [1. Bloodhound. 2. Dogs.] I. Title.

SF429.B6 M87 2003
636.753'6--dc21                                  2002074657

# Contents

# The Dog Family

Dogs and humans have been living together for thousands of years. Dogs were first tamed about 12,000 years ago. They were used as guards, hunters, and companions.

Today, about 400 different dog **breeds** exist. They can differ greatly in appearance. Some can weigh as much as 200 pounds (91 kg). Others are small enough to fit in the palms of your hands.

Despite these differences, all dogs belong to the same scientific **family**. It is called Canidae. This name comes from the Latin word *canis*, which means dog.

The Canidae family includes more than just **domestic** dogs. Foxes, jackals, coyotes, and wolves belong to this family, too. In fact, many people believe today's domestic dogs descended from wolves.

*Like the bloodhound, this red fox is a part of the Canidae family.*

# Bloodhounds

The bloodhound **breed** began hundreds of years ago. Monks at St. Hubert's **monastery** in Belgium bred these hounds as early as the 700s. There, they were known as St. Huberts. Eventually, bloodhounds were also bred in England. They first appeared in the United States more than 100 years ago.

Bloodhounds have an excellent sense of smell. Their ability to track a scent has aided people for many years. Originally, hunters used bloodhounds to sniff out **game**. More recently, they have been used to track lost people and escaped criminals.

Bloodhounds can follow a scent for miles. They can even smell a scent that is several days old. One such bloodhound, Nick Carter, became famous for his tracking abilities. In the early 1900s, Nick Carter tracked down more than 600 criminals in the United States.

*Many of today's scent hounds descended from the bloodhound's ancestors.*

# What They're Like

Bloodhounds are scent hounds. They are fairly large dogs, but they are good-natured animals. Bloodhounds are shy, calm, and gentle. They are good with children and other animals. For these reasons, they can make excellent pets.

Because they are so big, bloodhounds need plenty of space and lots of exercise. They love to track scents. They enjoy it so much that sometimes they don't pay any attention to their owners! This quality can sometimes make bloodhounds difficult to train.

Bloodhounds are friendly. They may bark at strangers, but they don't usually attack. They don't even attack the people or animals they track. Bloodhounds are also a little messy, because they often drool.

Bloodhounds can be stubborn, but they learn quickly.

# Coat and Color

The hair on a bloodhound's head and ears is soft. The rest of its coat is usually rougher. It can be black and tan, **liver** and tan, or solid red in color. Sometimes, a bloodhound can have white on its chest, its feet, or the tip of its tail.

A bloodhound's nose is black. Its droopy eyes can range in color from deep hazel to yellow. In dog shows, the **American Kennel Club** prefers bloodhounds with hazel eyes.

A bloodhound has thin, loose skin. This skin hangs in folds around the dog's head, neck, and mouth. When a bloodhound puts its head down, the skin falls over its forehead and the sides of its face. These folds help trap scents as the dog tracks.

Organizations such as the American Kennel Club hold competitions for bloodhounds and other purebred dogs.

# Size

The bloodhound is one of the larger **breeds** in the hound group. A male bloodhound stands about 26 inches (66 cm) tall at its shoulders. It can weigh between 90 and 110 pounds (41 and 50 kg). A female bloodhound is usually a bit smaller.

The bloodhound has a powerful, muscular body. It has strong legs. Its tail is thick, long, and set low on its body.

A bloodhound has a narrow head. Its **muzzle** is long and square. The nose has large nostrils. The eyes are set deep, and the ears are long and thin.

The bloodhound has a strong neck. Its back and shoulders are also strong. This allows it to follow a scent with its nose to the ground without tiring.

*The bloodhound's ability to track a scent is so accurate, it can be used as evidence in court in many U.S. states.*

# Care

Caring for a bloodhound is fairly easy. Its coat should be brushed a few times a week with a grooming glove or rubber brush. This will keep the coat shiny and clean. These supplies can be purchased at a local pet store.

A bloodhound's eyes and ears should be cleaned regularly. Gently wipe around the areas with a moist cotton ball. This will keep the dog's eyes and ears free of infection.

Bloodhounds and other big dogs sometimes suffer from **bloat**. A dog with bloat has a swollen stomach and is usually restless and uncomfortable. This condition can be fatal if it is not treated quickly by a **veterinarian**.

Your bloodhound should also visit the **veterinarian** for a checkup at least once a year. He or she can check your dog for illnesses and give it shots to prevent diseases. If you are not going to **breed** your dog, have the veterinarian **spay** or **neuter** it.

*Make sure your dog has its own place to sleep. Some dogs also like toys, such as rubber bones or squeaky toys.*

# Feeding

Dog food can be dry, moist, or semimoist. Most dogs will eat a high-quality, dry dog food. Others prefer to have some canned food mixed in with their dry food. To help prevent **bloat**, mix dry food with a little water to soften it.

Choose a type of food your dog enjoys and stick with it. Changes in diet should be made gradually to prevent stomach problems.

A bloodhound's daily food allowance should be divided into two meals. Two meals prevent the dog from eating too quickly. Eating or drinking too quickly, or exercising right after eating, may cause bloat.

Dogs need fresh, clean water every day. They also like treats. Give dogs treats only occasionally. This will keep them healthy.

Puppies need to eat more than adult dogs. Ask a veterinarian for tips on how much to feed your bloodhound.

# Things They Need

Bloodhounds need plenty of exercise. They love to go for long walks and follow scent trails. Always walk your bloodhound on a leash. Otherwise, it may take off after a scent. Playing ball or other games is also good exercise.

Bloodhounds need plenty of room to move around. They are happiest when they can play in a big, fenced-in yard. But they need protection from extremely hot or cold conditions. A sturdy doghouse will provide them with the protection they need.

Every dog should wear a collar with two tags. One tag shows the dog has had its shots. The other tag shows the dog's name and its owner's address and phone number. A dog can also have a **tattoo** or **microchip** for identification.

Bloodhounds are not good apartment dogs. They need a lot of space to sniff around.

# Puppies

Baby dogs are called puppies. A mother dog is **pregnant** for about nine weeks. Bloodhounds have about 10 puppies in a **litter**.

Puppies are born blind and deaf. Their eyes and ears will begin working when they are about two weeks old. They can walk at three weeks, and they are usually **weaned** at about seven weeks of age.

Puppies can be given away or sold when they are about eight weeks old. If you are going to buy a **purebred** puppy, make sure to buy it from a qualified **breeder**. Many puppies and older dogs are also available from the **Humane Society**.

It is important to take your puppy to the **veterinarian**. He or she will give your puppy the shots it needs to stay healthy. A puppy should start getting its shots when it is between six and eight weeks old.  A healthy bloodhound will live about 10 years.

Purebred dogs can cost anywhere from a few hundred to a few thousand dollars.

# Glossary

**American Kennel Club** - a club that studies, breeds, and exhibits purebred dogs.

**bloat** - a condition in which air gets trapped in a dog's stomach, causing pain, shock, and even death.

**breed** - a group of dogs sharing the same appearance and characteristics. A breeder is a person who raises dogs. Raising dogs is often called breeding them.

**domestic** - living with humans.

**family** - a group that scientists use to classify similar plants and animals. It ranks above a genus and below an order.

**game** - wild animals hunted for sport or food.

**Humane Society** - an organization that cares for and protects animals.

**litter** - all the puppies born at one time to a mother dog.

**liver** - a grayish, reddish-brown color.

**microchip** - a small computer chip. A veterinarian inserts the chip between a dog's shoulder blades. If the dog is lost, the Humane Society can scan the chip to find the dog's identification information and owners.

**monastery** - a place where monks live and work.

22

**muzzle** - an animal's nose and jaws.

**neuter** - to remove a male animal's reproductive parts.

**pregnant** - having one or more babies growing within the body.

**purebred** - an animal whose parents are both from the same breed.

**spay** - to remove a female animal's reproductive parts.

**tattoo** - a permanent design made on the skin. An owner can have an identification number tattooed on the leg of his or her dog.

**veterinarian** - a doctor who cares for animals.

**wean** - to accustom an animal to eating food other than its mother's milk.

# Web Sites

Would you like to learn more about bloodhounds? Please visit **www.abdopub.com** to find up-to-date Web site links about dog care and the bloodhound breed. These links are routinely monitored and updated to provide the most current information available.

# Index